Hi! Have you ever heard of the Common Good? That's great! It's really key that the bus driver believes in that. In other words:

Don't Let the Republican Drive the Bus!

by erich origen & gan golan

A PARODY FOR VOTERS

TEN SPEED PRESS

Berkeley

I'm counting on YOU!

Library of Congress Cataloging-in-Publication Data
is on file with the publisher.

ISBN 978-1-60774-392-7
eISBN 978-1-60774-393-4

Printed in China

Design by Erich Origen and Gan Golan

10 9 8 7 6 5 4 3 2 1

First Edition

True, I only like a few kinds of people.
But that's all we need in this great country of ours–*right!?*

Run over the little guy!

And unions!

And gay unions!

Teachers! Firefighters!
Veterans! Women...

Don't mind the bumps, folks!

Oops! Old man under the wheel! No more social security for you!

Probably had a victim mentality.

Take responsibility for me running you over!

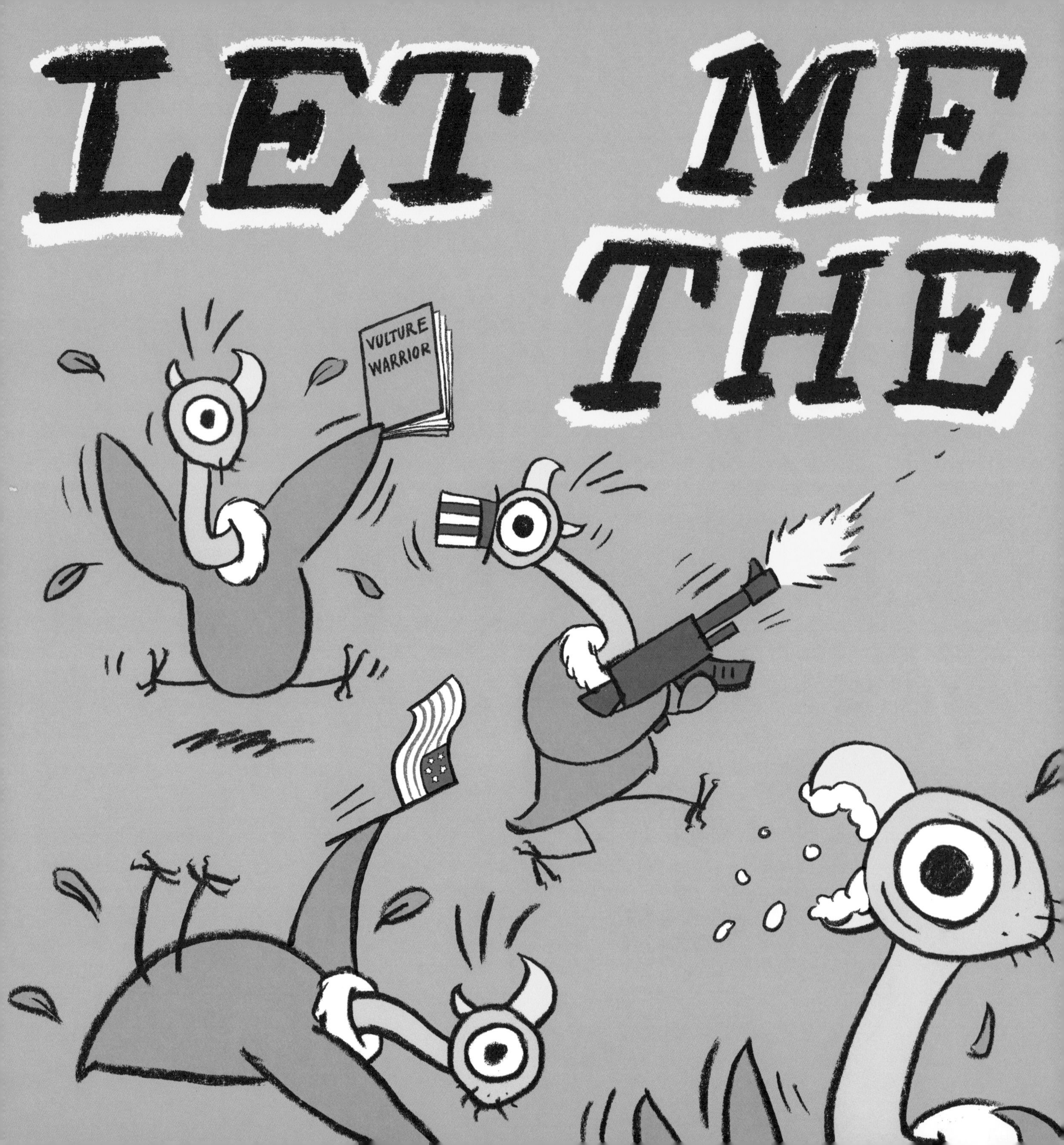
LET ME
THE
VULTURE WARRIOR

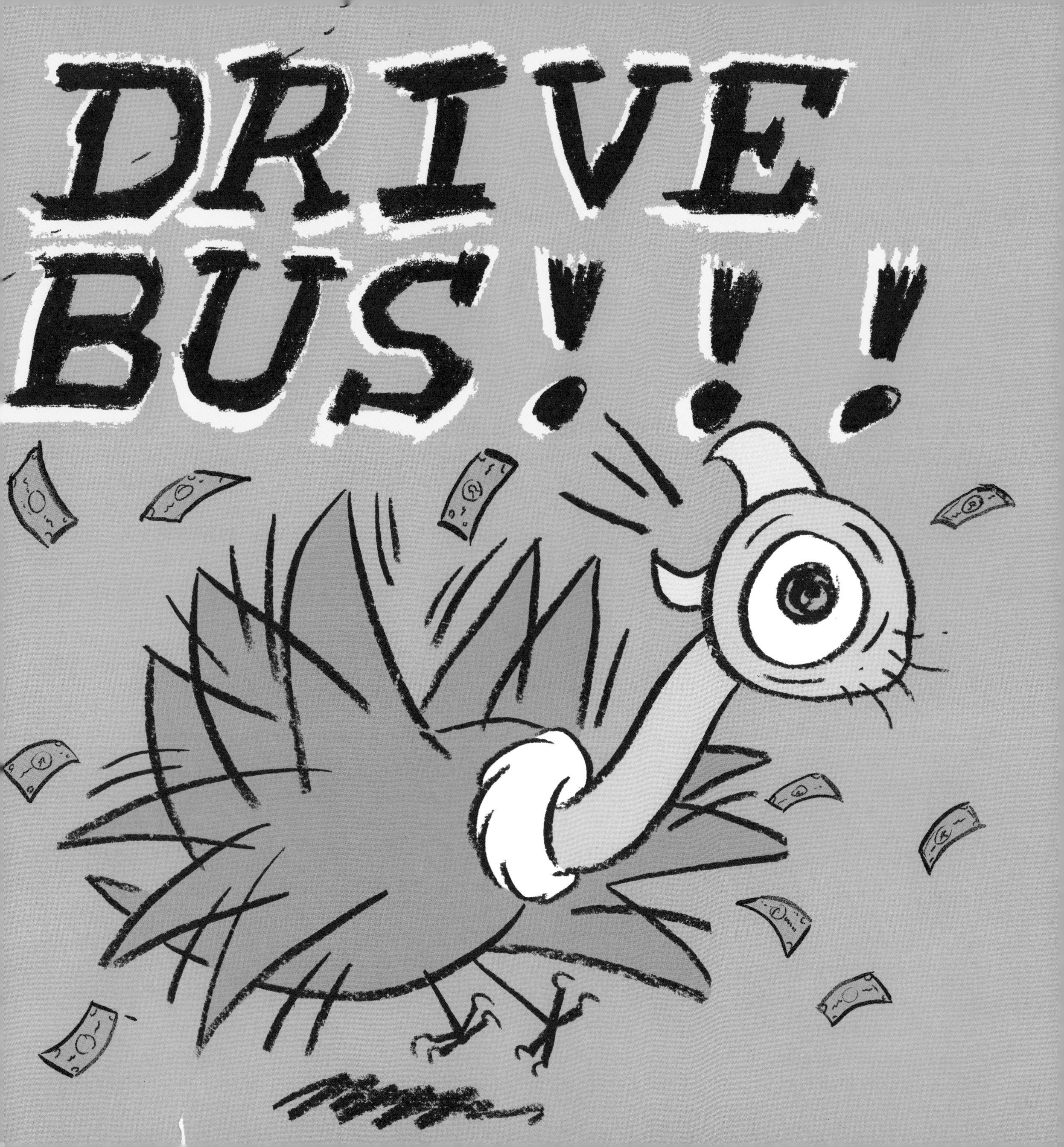
DRIVE
BUS!!!

Public-transit-using,
public-education-crusading,
public-radio-listening,
public-library-visiting,
public-park-picnicking,
gay-alien-loving
ELITISTS!

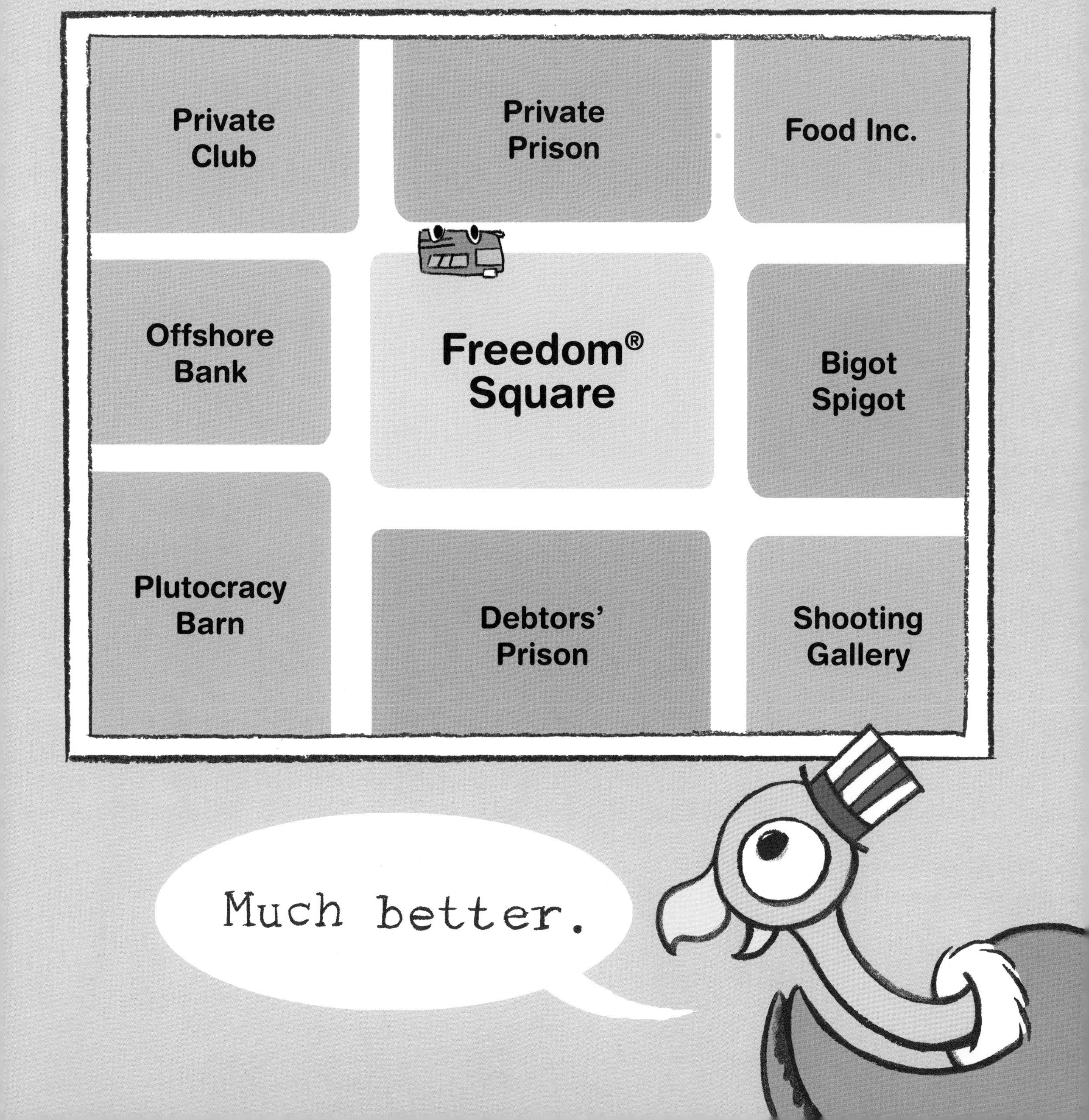
Private Club
Private Prison
Food Inc.
Offshore Bank
Freedom® Square
Bigot Spigot
Plutocracy Barn
Debtors' Prison
Shooting Gallery
Much better.

He did it!

Mmmm...tastes like chicken!

Afterword

Don't Let the Pigeon Drive the Bus! is the story of a creature putting his own impossible desires above everything and everyone, using all means necessary to achieve an end that is ridiculous and disastrous. Denied his impossible ambition, the bird grows angrier and has a full-blown tantrum. Such behavior is par for the course for your average three-year-old. But while a child's tantrum may be "developmentally appropriate," a rampaging id is more frightening in adults – and can have consequences that are far from cute.

Republicans want government jobs, but they hate government. They prefer "market-based solutions" – like the Great Depression. Yup, the Republicans were driving the bus just before the Great Crash of 1929. After that disaster, Americans kicked the party to the curb and demanded a New Deal. It worked. From the 1940s to the 1970s, America experienced its Great Prosperity. Ever since then, Republicans have attempted to rewrite the rules. Just like the pigeon in *Don't Let the Pigeon Drive the Bus!* they've tried everything to get us to hand over the keys. So charming, that bird.

The dominance of the Democratic species ended soon after the defeat of Jim Crow. Republicans smelled an opportunity and hatched the Southern Strategy, which has since migrated across the nation with wild success.

Republican survival is now fully dependent on the American population remaining bitterly divided against itself.

Today's Republicans are more bigoted and anti-intellectual than ever. They want us to take everything on faith, most importantly the idea that markets are self-regulating — a notion that even Alan Greenspan has called a "mistake." An unrestrained free-market utopia is an impossibility, and attempts to create one have resulted in bubble after bubble.

Not that the Democrats should get a free pass. Like Republicans, they've sold out to the casino-economy policies backed by Wall Street. They've joined the squawking of hawks, backed the indefinite caging of citizens, and flown with the Republican flock in pursuit of Juan Crow. Yet for all their faults, at least the Democrats profess to believe in the common good and occasionally make an effort at being the party of all Americans, not just a select few.

Ideologies get passed down from one vulture to the next via regurgitation. We hope this book helps inoculate you against this strain of bird flu. In the meantime, if you don't want to get thrown under it, then please...

DON'T LET THE REPUBLICAN DRIVE THE BUS!